LONGMAN AMERICAN BUSINESS ENGLISH SKILLS

EXCHANGING
INFORMATION
IN BUSINESS
GIVE & TAKE

Longman

ANNE AKAMATSU
Series editors Andrew Vaughan and Neil Heyen

Addison Wesley Longman Limited,
Edinburgh Gate, Harlow,
Essex CM20 2JE, England
and Associated Companies throughout the world.

First published 1994
Fourth impression 1998

Printed in China
EPC/04

ISBN 0 582 08419 9

Acknowledgements

We are grateful to the following for permission to reproduce copyright photographs:

The Image Bank for page 37; Images Colour Library for page 47; Longman Photographic Unit for pages 41–44; Telegraph Colour Library for page 28; Zefa Picture Library (UK) Ltd for pages 14 and 21.

Designed by Giles Davies

Illustrated by George Parkins

Cover Photograph by Longman Photographic Unit

Contents

About the Series

This text is one of a series of American English business textbooks designed for lower intermediate students. The titles in the series reflect some of the activities that students at this level are frequently asked to perform. The aim of the series is to provide support for specific areas of business performance rather than to improve overall language proficiency. The texts are ideal supplements to longer, more general courses, and can also be used individually in a short course, or in combination with each other to form a longer course.

We strongly feel that the most valuable resource in any Business English course is the students themselves. The role of the instructor in such a course is to draw on, and provide the language support for, the real life experiences and needs of the students. Through all of the texts we have tried to put the focus on the students' lives outside of the classroom. In our experience, the more connection that can be made between what goes on in the classroom and what happens on-the-job, the more successful a course will be.

About the Book

Give and Take is designed for lower intermediate students who use English in the workplace. It is based upon the actual experiences of students using English in their work, and teaches the language and functions they found most useful.

The six units in this book center around the happenings in three companies. Although specific businesses are named, the language and functions taught in each unit are applicable to students in a whole range of industries and occupations, and are suitable for any student who uses English in their work, either at home or abroad.

Each unit begins with a scenario introducing the business situation and characters. The scenario is followed by a dialogue which serves as a model of the language and functions taught in the unit. Further activities are designed to actively involve the student in the learning process by having them contribute the language they know, build upon that base, and practice what they have learned.

This book is best suited to classroom use but can also be used for self-study, as there is an answer key at the end of the book and an accompanying cassette tape.

The book can be used for intensive or extensive courses. It can also be used in conjunction with the other language tests in the series or such books as *Ready for Business* or *Functioning in Business*.

Using the Book

Although there are some common features, there is no standard pattern to the units. Given below are some suggestions for using the book.

Unit Introduction

Each unit begins with a *Unit Focus* box which lists the topics to be covered in the unit, and three *discussion questions*. The instructor can use the questions as a warm-up activity and as a way to learn what the students already know about the unit focus.

Following the discussion questions is a brief *scenario*, which introduces the company featured in the unit, the business situation and characters involved. The instructor should make sure that the students understand the scenario.

Pre-Listening

The scenario is followed by a pre-listening exercise which presents key vocabulary used in the unit. The instructor should check that students understand the vocabulary before proceeding with the activities.

Activity Work

With much of the activity work, there are no "correct" answers. As a result, students should spend time comparing and discussing their answers with each other (level permitting). Answers for the activities have been provided in the back of the book, but students should be made aware that some of the answers are samples only, and not necessarily the correct or best answers.

The length of time required to complete any activity depends on the level of the students and how much the instructor feels a particular activity needs to be exploited. Many of the activities calling for pair work can easily be expanded to include group or class discussions. Preparation for activities which require more student input can be assigned as homework, saving the discussion portions for class time.

The activity work begins with a listening cloze passage. This passage contains samples of the language focused on in the unit, introducing that language to the students in a business context. The instructor may want to allow the students to review the listening passage after completing several of the other activities. That would also be a good time to review the unit story.

Your Turn

This is probably the most important section in each unit. In this section the student tests out what was studied in the unit through participation in a role play. Role play exercises work best when students are fully prepared and clearly understand their roles, so the instructor should allow plenty of time for preparation and any questions the students may have.

Time

About four to five hours should be sufficient for each unit. Of course, this will vary depending on the students' level and the amount of time spent on discussions. The units can easily be broken down into several lessons and can therefore accommodate class periods of varying length.

Gathering Information

UNIT FOCUS
- Gathering Facts
- Asking For Opinions
- Restatement

How important is up-to-date information for your company? Where do you get your information from? Is it difficult to find information?

Comtec, a computer manufacturer based in Tokyo, is holding a meeting of its North American marketing staff. Marketing managers from Comtec sales offices in Canada, Mexico and the US have come to Tokyo to see a new computer series.

Match the words from the dialogue with the phrases on the right.

1. ___ a series   a. a particular product type

2. ___ a model   b. a display of products or services by various companies

3. ___ to introduce   c. to present something for the first time

4. ___ a show   d. a group of related products

Compare answers with your classmates and practice using the words in sentences.

Activity 1

Mr. Ito, the international marketing manager, is finishing his presentation of the new series.

Listen to the following dialogue and complete the missing passages.

MR. ITO: . . . So we are planning to release this new computer series in mid-spring, around April 15. Well, [1]_____ _____ of the series? Mr. Moran?

MR. MORAN: [2]_____. I especially like the portable model. You know, such a product is very important in our market and should do quite well.

MR. ITO: Mr. Garcia, [3]_____ well with your marketing plans?

MR. GARCIA: Yes, it does.

MR. ITO: [4]_____ of the models [5]_____ in Mexico?

MR. GARCIA: The first one you showed us will do well. Our customers will like the high quality.

MR. ITO: Ms. Cole, [6]_____ about the new series?

MS. COLE: Well, frankly, I'm disappointed. We don't have anything new here. We need new technology in the US market.

MR. GARCIA: Mr. Ito, [7]_____ at the last meeting that the design department was working on some new technology?

MR. ITO: Yes, they are, but development is taking more time than they expected.

MR. MORAN: Can they prepare something by spring?

MR. ITO: [8]_____. Maybe if we delayed releasing the series until June . . .

MS. COLE: But we can't wait. We have to introduce this new series at the trade show in March. It's the most important show of the year.

MR ITO: I see. I'll ask design to start making changes immediately.

MR. MORAN: [9]_____?

MR. ITO: I'll ask them to be finished by January. [10]_____

_____, Ms. Cole, will January be all right?

MS. COLE: That should be fine, if there aren't any delays.

Gathering Facts

When you need more than a yes or no answer, use open-ended questions.

Compare the two question-and-answer styles below.

Yes/No answers don't vary; they are either "yes" or "no"	Open-ended answers may vary
Q: Do you like the portable computer? A: No. Q: Is Ms. Cole arriving soon? A: Yes.	Q: Which computer do you like? A: I like the desktop model. Q: When is Ms. Cole arriving? A: At 5:20 p.m.

Activity 2

Change the yes/no questions into open-ended questions.

1. Can you speak English?

_____.

2. Are you from this area?

_____.

3. Do you travel overseas often?

_____.

4. Do you work for a large company?

_____.

5. Do you know much about computers?

_____.

Now write two more open-ended questions. Use all seven questions to interview a partner.

6. _____?

7. _____?

Activity 3

Introduce your partner from Activity 2 to the class. As you listen to the other introductions, complete the following table with the names of classmates.

Who?	
	Can speak English
	Is from this area
	Travels overseas often
	Works for a large company
	Knows much about computers

Now compare your results with the rest of the class. Does any of your information differ? What other information did you hear?

Asking for Opinions

Here are two expressions used to ask someone for an opinion.

How do you feel about ...
How do you feel about his marketing plan?

What do you think about ...
What do you think about the new office?

Activity 4 | *Use the preceding expressions to complete the question for each of the following answers. Then compare your work with a partner.*

1. _____ the new computer series?

I like it. It should sell well.

2. _____ the conference?

It's interesting, but a little too crowded.

3. _____ the new phone system?

It's too confusing! I can't figure it out.

4. _____ his idea?

I think it's good, but I want to study it some more.

Activity 5 | *On a sheet of paper write down several facts about yourself. Exchange this paper with a partner. On your partner's paper write down as many questions as you can about your partner's facts. When you have finished, ask your partner the questions you have written. Use yes/no, open-ended and opinion-asking question styles.*

Example:
Your partner writes: *I am thirty years old.*
You ask: *When is your birthday?* or *Did you just turn thirty?* or *How do you feel about being thirty?*

Restatement

During a conversation you will sometimes want to check that you understand what the speaker has said. You can do this by restating the speaker's ideas in your own words.

Here are two phrases you can use to restate your ideas.

So, what you mean is . . .
In other words . . .

Study the following sample conversation.

A: . . . The customer doesn't like our offer.
B: *So, what you mean is,* our price is too high.
A: No, the price is OK but our one-year warranty is too short.

B: *In other words,* if we offer a longer warranty, they'll buy the product.

A: Yes, that's right.

Activity 6

Mr. Ito and Ms. Cole are discussing preparations for the spring trade show.

Together with a partner read the dialogue and fill in the missing phrases.

MR. ITO: Well, Ms. Cole, the last time we met you told me about your plans for the trade show. How are your preparations going?

MS. COLE: Well, we're having a little trouble.

MR. ITO: ¹_____, you're falling behind schedule?

MS. COLE: No, not yet. But we can't complete our preparations until this new series is completed. We need sample computers from this series to finish training our staff.

MR. ITO: In other words, ²_____

_____.

MS. COLE: That's right. We'd like to receive them by January.

MR. ITO: Well, design needs time to complete their work, so I think January is too early. How do you feel about a later date?

MS. COLE: ³_____ in February? The first or second week of February would be OK.

MR. ITO: All right, I'll do what I can.

MS. COLE: Thank you, I really appreciate your help.

Listen to the dialogue and compare your answers to the tape. Remember, the taped dialogue uses possible answers. Your answers may differ slightly.

Activity 7

Rewrite the following statements.

Example: People need products which don't cost a lot, but all of our products are expensive.

In other words, we need to lower our prices.

Example: Many people don't understand technology, so they buy things that are easy to use.

What you mean is, low-tech items are popular.

1. I should have finished this report already, but I got too busy.

_____

2. These cars aren't popular. People think they're unsafe.

_____

3. Our stock of this computer is a little low. It has sold very well.

_____

4. We have to finish this report by Monday. That's when Mr. Carlson arrives.

_____

5. I ordered those lap-tops four months ago but I haven't received them yet. Our big sales promotion starts next week.

_____

6. She bought this car. It has a good safety record.

_____

Select some of the restatements and take turns reading them to a partner. As you listen to your partner, try to guess which statements your partner rewrote.

Your Turn   *You are going to interview a partner. Choose one of the following topics: 1) Your Job   2) Your Co-workers   3) Your Company*

A	B
Interview your partner about the topic you have chosen. During the interview you should find out your partner's opinions and ideas on the topic. Remember to use restatement where necessary. Before beginning, think about or write down different types of questions to ask during the interview. Use some yes/no, some open-ended and some opinion questions.	You are going to be interviewed by your partner. Before beginning, make a few notes about what you might say in the interview.

When you finish, change roles. Then choose a new topic and repeat the role play.

13

Polite Speech

UNIT FOCUS
■ Asking Questions
■ Entering Conversations
■ Tone

How important is politeness in business? Is politeness less important than it used to be? Why or why not?

Luna, an American watch manufacturer, buys watch parts from Pacific Precision of Hong Kong. To meet a rush order, Luna has asked Pacific Precision to increase production and complete 140,000 units in seven weeks.

It is now the end of week three, and only 39,000 units have been shipped. Managers from Luna and Pacific Precision are meeting in Hong Kong to discuss the slow production.

Match the words from the dialogue with the phrases on the right.

1. ____ a shift   a. a single item

2. ____ a supervisor   b. missing something, not enough

3. ____ a unit   c. a regular work period

4. ____ to be short   d. someone who manages a group of workers

Compare answers with your classmates and practice using the words in sentences.

Activity 1

Luna purchasing manager Louis Bogart and Pacific Precision production manager Vincent Chang are discussing their production problem. Joining in the meeting are their quality control officers, Frank Segal from Luna and John Lee from Pacific Precision.

Listen to the following dialogue and complete the missing passages.

MR. BOGART: I know it's difficult, but at the end of seven weeks we are going to be short 49,000 units unless you speed up your production.

MR. CHANG: [1]_____? I don't think it's possible.

MR. BOGART: Well, you can add another work shift. By adding a shift you would . . .

MR. LEE: [2]_____, Mr. Bogart, but we have already done that. We've changed from a twelve-hour shift to a sixteen-hour shift. Almost all of our factory employees are working overtime.

MR. SEGAL: [3]_____, but I think I have an idea.

MR. CHANG: [4]_____?

MR. SEGAL: Well, if you hire more workers you can run the plant for twenty-four hours, using three shifts.

MR. CHANG: I'm sorry, I can't agree with that.

MR. BOGART: [5]_____? It sounds good to me.

MR. CHANG: The problem is a matter of time. We would need time to train new workers on the machines.

MR. SEGAL: What kind of training program do you have now?

MR. LEE: After two days of training, each new employee works with a supervisor for two more days, before working alone.

MR. BOGART: It might be possible to reduce training time.

MR. CHANG: ^{6}_____?

MR. BOGART: We could skip the two days of supervision.

MR. CHANG: No, I'm sorry, the supervision is too important.

MR. SEGAL: ^{7}_____, but ^{8}_____ cut that stage?

MR. LEE: We've found that most mistakes happen during the first week of work. Two days of supervision greatly reduces the number of mistakes.

MR. SEGAL: But that also increases the production time.

MR. CHANG: Yes, in the short term, but in the long term it saves time because quality is higher.

Asking Questions

One error many language learners make is asking questions which are too abrupt, or sudden and short. Abrupt questions can seem rude, and may make the listener feel uncomfortable.

Compare the two question types in the table below.

	Abrupt	**Less abrupt**
The parts won't be available until next week.	Q: Why?	Q: Why will they be delayed?
I can't join you for dinner tonight, but maybe I could meet you another time.	Q: When?	Q: When would be a good time for you?

One way to make questions less abrupt is to make the questions longer. Sometimes we change the words completely.

Activity 2

Rewrite the following questions to make them less abrupt.

1. You need to speed up your production. (How?)

   _____

2. Excuse me, but I think I have an idea. (What?)

   _____

3. I'm sorry, I can't agree with that. (Why not?)

   _____

4. It might be possible to reduce training time. (How?)

   _____

16

Activity 3 | *Use the following questions to interview a partner. Change each abrupt question so that it is less abrupt. Listen carefully to your partner's answers. You may have to change your questions during the interview.*

1. Do you enjoy your job?
2. Why?/Why not?
3. Have you ever had a different job?
4. Where?/Why not?
5. Do you meet with customers as part of your job?
6. Who?/Why?
7. Have you ever been overseas?
8. Where?/Why not?
9. Do you want to travel overseas?
10. Where?/Why not?

Entering Conversations

When you enter into an ongoing conversation you need to get the speaker's attention, but you also need to be polite.

Here are two expressions used to enter a conversation.

Excuse me, but...
Sorry to interrupt, but...

Activity 4 *Work with a partner to make a list of other expressions you can use to enter into a conversation. Order the expressions from most polite to least polite.*

1. _____

2. _____

3. _____

4. _____

Compare your list with the rest of the class. Are any of the expressions too polite? Too rude?

Activity 5 *Work with a partner to complete the following dialogue with the expressions you learned in Activity 4.*

Five people are deciding where they will have their sales meeting next year.

MR. SATO: Well, everyone in Tokyo agrees that the annual sales meeting should be in Singapore next year.

MS. BROWN: Should we have it in November again?

MR. SATO: If that's all right with everyone. It's a good time for us.

MR. CHEN: [1]_____, but why do you want the meeting in Singapore?

MS. BROWN: Well, we had it there this year and it went very well.

MR. NAKAMURA: Yes, the facilities were very good.

MR. LIEST: [2]_____, but we were hoping that the meeting would be in Europe next year. We think that the meeting should be at a different sales office every year.

MR. SATO: Yes, but we did have the meeting in Bonn two years ago. And Singapore is very convenient.

MR. CHEN: [3]_____, but what about Hong Kong? We had the meeting there four years ago and it went very well.

Now meet with another pair of students and compare your finished dialogues. Do both dialogues use polite language?

Activity 6

Work in a small group. Each of you should choose one of the following statements.

1. Our company should have a shorter work week.
2. A large company is an inefficient company.
3. High technology creates too much stress in the office.
4. A company should have a large number of foreign workers.
5. We need more women managers in business.
6. Older employees are better employees.

Read your statement to the group and give at least two reasons to support it.

Ask others for their opinions about your statement and reasons. Try to use the language you learned to ask questions and to enter into a conversation.

Tone

Often *how* someone says something is just as important as *what* they say. Tone is the meaning carried by a person's voice, such as happiness, anger, and worry. A pleasant tone can make an abrupt question polite, and an angry tone can make "Excuse me" seem rude.

Activity 7

Listen to the tape and identify the tone you hear each time the speaker reads the sentence: "Where have you been?" Choose your answer from the following list.

(A) angry   (H) happy   (W) worried   (I) interested   (N) neutral

1. _____   2. _____   3. _____   4. _____   5. _____

Activity 8

Pacific Precision has decided to hire more workers. John Lee and Frank Segal are meeting to discuss the new employee training schedule.

Listen to the dialogue and select a tone to match each underlined phrase. Choose your answer from the following list.

(A) angry   (H) happy   (W) worried   (I) interested   (N) neutral

MR. SEGAL: I still don't understand why we can't cut the supervision stage . . .

MR. LEE: We can't cut the two days of supervision. [1](___)

MR. SEGAL: But we have to cut something. [2](___) Can we cut the training by a day and still get quality work?

MR. LEE: Hmmm . . . . that's an option, [3](___) but I'm afraid that cutting the training time will leave us with product defects and more delays!

MR. SEGAL: No, I mean that instead of cutting the overall training time, we increase the supervision time to three days.

MR. LEE: I'm sorry, I don't see your point. [4](___)

MR. SEGAL: I mean, we should have one day of machine training and three days of supervision. That way the workers can start production twenty-four hours earlier.

MR. LEE: Hmmm. But I'm still worried about the quality. [5](___) If we do this, we should increase the inspection ratio.

MR. SEGAL: Yes, that's not a bad idea.

MR. LEE: OK. I think we have a deal. [6](___) One day of machine training and three days of supervision.

MR. SEGAL: Great! [7](___)

Activity 9

Work with a partner. Practice the tones listed above by reading the following model sentence out loud. Each time you read the sentence, your partner should guess which tone you are using.

Model sentence: "How long will you be in Paris?"

Your Turn

Work in small groups for the following situation. Use the language you have learned to ask questions and enter into the conversation. Be aware of the meaning your tone of voice can carry.

Your company has decided to open a new office overseas. You and the members of your group are meeting together to select the new office site. You must:
1. make a list of at least four possible office locations
2. agree on a rank order of the locations, from best to worst

When you have completed the role play, compare your results with the rest of the class.

Persuading Your Audience

UNIT FOCUS
- Introducing and Supporting Ideas
- Making Recommendations
- Giving Opinions

What makes someone a persuasive speaker? Do you consider yourself persuasive? Would you like to be more persuasive?

Davis, Incorporated is an American printer manufacturer. Staff members from purchasing, design and quality assurance are meeting to select a supplier for the circuit board to be used in Davis' newest printer, the DV6700.

Match the words from the dialogue with the phrases on the right.

1. ____ a factor   a. a point or idea to think about

2. ____ slightly   b. a holdup, to be late

3. ____ a delay   c. reliable, often used

4. ____ regular   d. a little bit

Compare answers with your classmates and practice using the words in sentences.

Activity 1

Beth Ellis from purchasing at Davis is finishing her presentation about circuit board suppliers. Mark Green from design and Bob Fisher from quality assurance have joined her in this meeting.

Listen to the following dialogue and complete the missing passages.

MS. ELLIS: The DV6700 is our most important printer this year, with our newest technology. Because of this, [1]_____ we should make quality the most important factor in choosing a circuit board for this printer.

MR. FISHER: We've tested samples from Olsen Electronics and Marin Technics. Both samples are good, but Olsen's quality is slightly better.

MR. GREEN: [2]_____ that we also need to consider cost. How do the two companies compare?

MS. ELLIS: Both companies are offering the same price, but there is one difference. Because we are a regular customer, Olsen will be very flexible with their production schedule. [3]_____ we should choose Olsen, [4]_____ their price is OK and we need the flexibility they offer.

MR. FISHER: Olsen? But we always have problems with Olsen when we use them. There are production delays . . .

MR. GREEN: Yes, but according to your test data, Olsen's quality is better than Marin Technics'.

MR. FISHER: I said that the Olsen circuit board is slightly better. Frankly, [5]_____ that Marin Technics is the best choice, [6]_____ our engineers can always give them some instructions for improvements.

MR. GREEN: Well, [7]_____ that it would be a lot easier to use Olsen, like we did before.

MR. FISHER: No, 8_____ use Marin Technics,

9_____ their quality can be improved, their price is good and they won't give us any holdups like Olsen always does.

MS. ELLIS: Hmmm, 10_____. Also, if we do decide to use the DV6700 circuit board in our other models, Marin should be able to . . .

Introducing and Supporting Ideas

When introducing an idea into a conversation it is important to give reasons to support it.

> **I think that** Marin Technics is best **because** their quality can be improved and their price is good.
>
> **It seems to me that** Olsen is a good choice, **because** we have used them before.

Activity 2

Listed below are several ideas. Tell a partner what you think about each idea, and why. Write your partner's comments in the chart.

Example: I don't agree with the first idea because I think that children need to study traditional subjects.

Idea	Agree	Disagree	Reason
Children need computer training in elementary school.			
Too much technology is dangerous.			
Price is more important than quality.			
Simple products are the best products.			

Compare your chart with the rest of the class. Does everyone share the same ideas?

Making Recommendations

A recommendation is an idea which suggests that something *should* or *should not* be done. Reasons to support your recommendation can come before or after the recommendation itself.

> **I think we should** choose Olsen **because** they are flexible.
>
> **Because** they are flexible, **I think we should** choose Olsen.

Activity 3

Study the following sample conversations and underline each recommended action.

1. A: I think we should buy this computer because the price is just right.
   B: But prices might drop again soon, so I think we should wait.

2. A: Because Mr. Burne is leaving tomorrow, we should talk with him today.
   B: OK, but we shouldn't take a lot of his time because he's very busy.

Activity 4

Together with a partner prepare one or two recommendations for change in your class or workplace. Prepare reasons to support each recommendation.

Recommendations	Reasons
1. _____	_____
_____	_____
2. _____	_____
_____	_____

Now discuss your ideas with the rest of the class. Did anyone have the same recommendations? Who had the best reasons to support their recommended changes?

Giving Opinions

Opinions are made up of your ideas, recommendations, and feelings. When you want to express an opinion, you can use these expressions:

Strongest	I definitely think/feel that (he is wrong).
	I really think/feel that (we should study this more).
	I think/feel that (we should go).
Weakest	I tend to think/feel that (we should invite them).

Activity 5

Rank the following opinions from strong to weak. Number 1 is the strongest, number 5 the weakest.

_____ I feel that you haven't studied this enough.

_____ I definitely think they will agree.

_____ I tend to feel that it's a good idea.

_____ I really feel that she will like this.

_____ I think this is a good report.

Activity 6

Beth Ellis is on the telephone with Jack Vargas of Marin Technics. She has called to tell him that Davis has chosen his company as the new circuit board supplier.

Listen to the following dialogue and complete the missing passages.

MR. VARGAS: Jack Vargas speaking.

MS. ELLIS: Jack, this is Beth Ellis from Davis. I have some good news for you. We've finished our evaluation and have decided to use your circuit board.

MR. VARGAS: Great! How large an order will you need?

MS. ELLIS: Before we do that, there are a few conditions we need to discuss.

MR. VARGAS: OK.

MS. ELLIS: The first condition concerns production. How do you feel about giving us a more flexible production schedule?

MR. VARGAS: Well, [1]_____.
We've done that sort of thing before.

MS. ELLIS: Good. Our other concern is the quality. We'd like you to accept some technical instructions from our engineers. What do you think?

MR. VARGAS: Hmmm. [2]_____ there'll be some problems. Can we set up a meeting between your engineering staff and mine? [3]_____ we should discuss this.

MS. ELLIS: [4]_____. And listen, Jack, don't worry too much about this. [5]_____ we've made the right choice by selecting Marin Technics.

[6]_____ after a few minor changes we'll have a fine product.

MR. VARGAS: I'm happy to hear you say that. Let's look at our calendars and set up that meeting. . . .

Activity 7

How do you feel about giving your opinion? Does it make you feel uncomfortable or do you like it? Use the following survey to interview a partner. Add two questions of your own to the survey before you begin.

Questions	Yes	No
1. Do you like to be asked for your opinion?		
2. Do you feel embarrassed when you have to give your opinion in front of many people?		
3. Do you ask other people for their opinions?		
4. Do you sometimes tell people, "I have no opinion"?		
5. If your opinion is different from your boss's, will you say so?		
6.		
7.		

Now compare your results with the rest of the class. Did everyone have the same opinions? Did your partner express any strong or weak opinions?

Your Turn

Divide into two groups. Each group must do all three parts of the activity.

Part One
Your company is studying job satisfaction and your group is taking a survey of the employees. As a group, make a list of questions about working life. Use the following phrases:

What do you think about . . .?

How do you feel about . . .?

Example: What do you think about working overtime?

Part Two
Now each member of your group should find a partner in the other group. Take turns asking questions to your partner and record their responses. Place a ✓ next to opinions they express strongly.

Part Three
Return to your original group and compare your results. Report your findings to the class.

Based on the findings of both groups, what recommendations for change in the workplace can you make?

Tasks and Requests

UNIT FOCUS
- **Explaining a Process**
- **Making Requests**
- **Accepting and Refusing Requests**

Have you ever been in charge of a group or project team? Would you find it easy or hard to manage a group? Why?

Comtec USA, a subsidiary of the computer manufacturer Comtec Japan, is preparing for an important trade show. Mr. Kenzo Ito, the international marketing manager from Tokyo, and managers from the Los Angeles office are meeting to discuss preparations for the show.

Pre-Listening

Match the words from the dialogue with the phrases on the right.

1. ____ features   a. to give someone a specific job

2. ____ to assign   b. a show or demonstration

3. ____ a display   c. a job, something to be done

4. ____ a task   d. special qualities

Compare answers with your classmates and practice using the words in sentences.

Activity 1

Mr. Ito has just finished introducing the company's new products to the Los Angeles management team. Ms. Baker, a marketing manager, is going to organize the trade show preparation.

Listen to the following dialogue and complete the missing passages.

MR. ITO: . . . Those are the new products and their features. Now I'd like us to discuss our preparation for the upcoming trade show. Ms. Baker?

MS. BAKER: Thank you, Mr. Ito. We have four steps to complete today.

^{1}_____, we need to assign tasks; who will be responsible

for which activities. ^{2}_____ we need to discuss how much

room each product will have. ^{3}_____, I'd like us to break up and work in groups for a few hours.

^{4}_____ , I'd like to meet again this afternoon to discuss our progress. Any questions? All right, let's start with the assignments. Ms. Cole, we'd like you to take care of the personal computer display.

MS. COLE: ^{5}_____. I have to be in New York at that time. I'd like to have Mr. Ford take my place.

MS. BAKER: Mr. Ford, is that all right with you?

MR. FORD: ^{6}_____.

MS. BAKER: Mr. Ito, ^{7}_____?
MR. ITO: Sure.

MS. BAKER: OK, Ms. Meyer, ^{8}_____ the printer team.

MS. MEYER: ^{9}_____. My staff has already started preparations.

MS. BAKER: Good, All right, last on the list is systems products. Mr. Miller, I'd like you to take care of that.

MR. MILLER: [10]_____. Can Mr. Phillips work with me?

MS. BAKER: Oh, yes, that's a good idea.

Explaining a Process

When you explain a process it is important that you clearly state the proper order of each step in the process.

One way to show order is to use ordinal numbers.

First, we have to contact our customers and show them our new products.

Second, we answer their questions.

Third, we take their orders.

Another way to order steps is to use language such as *next, then, after that, finally.*

Next we need to contact our factories.

After that we plan a production schedule.

Finally, we contact the customers again.

Most people combine both methods to produce a clear and interesting description.

First, we have to contact our customers and show them our new products and **then** we answer their questions. **Next** we take their orders. The **fourth** step we take is to contact our factories, and **after that** we plan a production schedule. **Finally**, we contact our customers again.

Activity 2

Listen as Ms. Cole describes the process of setting up a display for the trade show. Number each piece of the dialogue to put it in order.

A. _____ Make sure that everything works properly.

B. _____ Move our products to the display area and set them up.

C. _____ Arrange food for the customers.

D. _____ Set up the display area shelves and tables.

E. _____ Set up an information table.

Activity 3

Most people have a regular process or routine they follow every day when they arrive at work. Use the following questions to interview a partner about their work routine. Record your partner's answers next to the questions.

Daily Work Routine	
What time do you usually arrive at work?	
What is the first thing you do when you arrive?	
What do you do after that?	
What do you do next?	
When do you eat lunch?	
What do you do after lunch?	
What is the last thing you do at work each day?	
What is the most important thing you do at work each day?	

Activity 4

Think of one process that you have to do in your work, such as setting up a computer, writing a report, or planning a trip. Describe this process to a partner, using the language for describing a process. You can start by saying:

I'm going to describe how I . . .

When you are finished, listen to your partner describe a process. Check your understanding of their process with questions and a restatement in your own words.

Making Requests

A process can involve many tasks. When you want someone to complete a task, you can use these patterns to make your request.

> **We need you to** write the finance report.
>
> **Could you** get Ms. Cole, please?
>
> **I would like you to** call Mr. Johnson.
>
> **Please** take this to the sales department.
>
> **Can you** lend me your calculator?

Activity 5

Write a request for each of the following situations.

1. Your pen has stopped working. You want to use your friend's pen.

   _____.

2. You have to finish a report your boss needs today. You have a meeting with a customer at 3:00 p.m. You would like your co-worker to finish the report for you.

   _____.

3. You are taking a business trip to Peru next month. Your co-worker speaks Spanish, and you would like her to tutor you before you go.

   _____.

4. You forgot your wallet at home this morning. You want to borrow some money so you can buy lunch.

   _____.

5. You don't understand a new software system. You want someone to explain it to you.

   _____.

Now practice making your requests with a partner. When you have completed the requests above, continue with some ideas of your own.

Accepting and Refusing Requests

The simplest way to accept a request is to say "Yes" or "All right." When you accept a request, it is a good time to ask any questions you have.

Example: A: Mr. Miller, I'd like you to take care of the systems products.
               B: All right. Can I work together with Mr. Phillips on that?

When you have to refuse a request, it is polite to say "I'm sorry, but I can't..." or "I'm afraid I can't..." and give a reason why you can not accept the request.

Example: A: Ms. Cole, we'd like you to take care of the personal computer display.
               B: I'm sorry, but I can't. I have to be in New York at that time.

Activity 6

Mr. Ito asks Ms. Baker for some help.

Listen to the following dialogue and complete the missing passages.

MR. ITO: Ms. Baker, can you help me?

MS. BAKER: [1]_____. What can I do for you?

MR. ITO: I have to buy some souvenirs to take back to Japan, and I don't know what to buy. I need you to give me some advice.

MS. BAKER: Sure. [2]_____?

MR. ITO: My co-workers.

MS. BAKER: OK. Well, California wine is one idea.

MR. ITO: That sounds nice. Can you recommend a special brand?

MS. BAKER: [3]_____. I don't know much about wine. You should ask Ms. Cole.

MR. ITO: OK, I'll do that. There's one more thing. I'd like you to get everyone together for a short meeting this afternoon.

MS. BAKER: [4]_____. Both Mr. Ford and Ms. Cole are out this afternoon. Could you make it tomorrow morning?

MR. ITO: [5]_____. That'll be fine.

Activity 7 | *For each of the following requests, write an acceptance or a refusal. For each acceptance, write a question. For each refusal, write a reason why you cannot accept the request.*

1. I'd like you to work overtime tonight.

Acceptance: _____

Question: _____

2. We need you to go to Sydney next Monday.

Refusal: _____

Reason: _____

3. Ms. Meyer would like you to pick up Mr. Hashimoto at the airport.

Acceptance: _____

Question: _____

4. Can you join us for dinner tomorrow?

Refusal: _____

Reason: _____

Now meet with a partner and take turns making the above requests and accepting and refusing them.

Activity 8 | *You are going on a business trip for one week. Write down at least three tasks you will need your co-workers to do for you while you are gone. Ask your classmates to complete these tasks. When someone agrees to a request, write their name next to the task. If they refuse, find out why.*

Task	Who?
1. _____	_____
2. _____	_____
3. _____	_____

Your Turn

You are going to have a meeting with several of your classmates. Work in groups of three to five people.

> You and your group members work together in the general affairs department of the same company. Next week some directors are coming to visit your office and your group has to plan a schedule for the visitors. You must:
>
> 1. plan a schedule
> 2. decide what must be done to make the schedule successful
> 3. assign tasks to each group member
>
> The directors will be arriving at noon on Sunday and will leave the following Wednesday evening. They will have meetings every day from 9 a.m. to 2 p.m. The remainder of their time is free for you to schedule.

When you have completed your role play, introduce your group's schedule to the class. Talk about the tasks involved and who will complete them.

Agreement and Disagreement

UNIT FOCUS
- **Agreement and Disagreement**
- **Understanding and Agreement**
- **Body Language**

Do you often have disagreements in your meetings? Do you find it easy to tell people that you disagree with them? What do you do if people disagree with you?

Luna, an American watch manufacturer, recently asked Pacific Precision, its Hong Kong parts supplier, to greatly increase production to complete a special order. Pacific Precision had to make many changes in its production process to do this.

Now Luna needs another rapid order. Managers from Luna and Pacific Precision are meeting in Hong Kong to discuss this second order of watch parts.

Match the words from the dialogue with the phrases on the right.

1. ____ to break even   a. to operate or use

2. ____ freight   b. fair and agreeable

3. ____ reasonable   c. to recover costs, to get back what
                                     you put in

4. ____ to run   d. goods, products to be shipped

Compare answers with your classmates and practice using the words in sentences.

Activity 1

Louis Bogart and Vincent Chang are discussing the new order. Mr. Chang says he must increase his price.

Listen to the following dialogue and complete the missing passages.

MR. BOGART: This watch has been very popular, so we'd like you to supply an additional 100,000 units this month.

MR. CHANG: [1]_____. That's good news for us, but there is one problem.

MR. BOGART: What's that?

MR. CHANG: This increased schedule we're running has caused production costs to increase. At our last inspection we found that defects have doubled.

MR. BOGART: Well, [2]_____ your situation but your new workers should know their jobs by now. You shouldn't have any more problems.

MR. CHANG: [3]_____. Even if the workers improve, we can only hope to break even on this new order.

MR. BOGART: But if you increase your price we'll have to increase ours and we'll both lose business.

MR. CHANG: [4]_____, but we can't continue with the current situation.

MR. BOGART: There has to be something we can do to solve this problem.

MR. CHANG: Well, if you can give us a larger order, about 200,000 units, then we can keep our price low for you.

MR. BOGART: An extra 100,000? No, I'm sorry. I mean, [5]_____

_____, but [6]_____

_____.

MR. CHANG: How about air freight? If you pay for air freight, we can return to our normal production schedule and still deliver the order on time.

MR. BOGART: No, I'm sorry, [7]_____.
The cost is too high.

Levels of Agreement and Disagreement

In every language there are many levels of agreement and disagreement. You can completely agree or disagree with an idea, or partially agree or disagree.

Activity 2 | *Listed below are various expressions of agreement and disagreement. Where would you place each expression on the scale of agreement? Write a letter next to each expression.*

A	B	C	D	E

Completely agree ⟵_____⟶ **Completely disagree**

1. ____ I tend to disagree...

2. ____ Generally I agree, but...

3. ____ I'm sorry, I have to disagree.

4. ____ Exactly.

5. ____ I'm not so sure...

6. ____ I don't know...

7. ____ I'm afraid I disagree...

8. ____ I think so, too.

9. ____ I tend to agree, but...

10. ____ I'm sorry, I can't agree with that.

Activity 3 | *Complete the following statement with a partner.*

I think that...

Example: I think that everyone in business should study foreign languages.

You and your partner should each survey some of your classmates and record whether they agree or disagree with your statement. When you have finished, meet with your partner and compare your results.

Name	Completely Agree				Completely Disagree
	A	B	C	D	E

Understanding and Agreement

Many language learners confuse expressions of *agreement* with expressions of *understanding*. It is important to learn how to show that you understand what has been said, and whether you agree or disagree.

Here are some expressions which show understanding.

I see.	I understand.
I see your point.	I see what you mean.

To avoid confusion, you can combine an expression of understanding with an expression of agreement or disagreement.

Examples: I see, but I'm afraid I can't agree.
I understand, and I completely agree.
I see what you mean, but I tend to disagree.
I see your point, and generally I agree, but . . .

Activity 4 *Meet with a group and discuss your statements from Activity 3. During your discussions use the language above to show that you understand and agree or disagree with the others in your group.*

Body Language

Like tone of voice, your body language can add to or change the meaning of what you say.

Activity 5 | *Read the following descriptions of body language. What is the meaning of each "expression" in your culture? Write the meaning in the space provided. Compare your answers with the rest of the class when you are finished.*

Example: LISTENER: arms folded across chest, slight frown

The listener is angry or bored.

Description   **Meaning**

1. SPEAKER: posture relaxed, gesturing

_____

_____

2. SPEAKER: pointing at the
   listener, frowning

_____

_____

3. LISTENER: smiling, arms
   folded across chest

_____

_____

4. LISTENER: leaning forward
in chair, closely
watching speaker

_____

_____

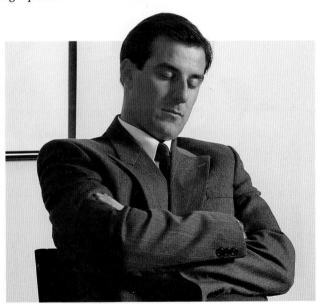

5. LISTENER: leaning back in
chair, arms folded, eyes
closed

_____

_____

*Now try to guess the meaning for each expression in English.
Compare your answers with your instructor and those in the
answer key.*

Mr. Bogart and Mr. Chang are meeting the next day.

As you listen to the following dialogue, write the letter of the matching picture next to each piece of conversation.

MR. BOGART: I'm sorry, but the head office wouldn't agree to an order for 200,000 units at this time.

MR. CHANG: But we simply can't continue the current production without a price increase.

MR. BOGART: Well, there must be some way . . .

MR. CHANG: There is air freight.

1. ___

MR. BOGART: I can't agree with that. The costs are simply too high. Look, we're depending on you to get us that next 100,000 at a reasonable cost.

MR. CHANG: Reasonable? Look at these charts. Since last month defects have risen sharply. This Luna order is costing us profits and customers.

2. ___

MR. BOGART: All right, look, let's not argue. We'll find a way to make this work. Maybe we can get you a larger order.

MR. CHANG: What do you have in mind?

3. ___

MR. BOGART: Well, I know we can't give you a 200,000 unit order. But maybe we can do 150,000.

MR. CHANG: Hmm.

MR. BOGART: What do you think?

MR. CHANG: With that size of order, I might be able to keep the costs down. Can you really do this?

4. ___

MR. BOGART: Yes.

MR. CHANG: Then you have a deal!

5. ___

Activity 7 *Work with a partner to write an adjective or short phrase which describes the body language shown in each illustration in Activity 6.*

Compare your descriptions with the rest of the class. Did everyone use the same adjective for each illustration?

Your Turn

Luna will send one of their people to Pacific Precision as a trainee next year to study Cantonese and Pacific Precision's production system. Four people have been recommended as trainees.

Jack Rivard   purchasing, an engineer, speaks English, French and some Spanish, single, 34

Marie Grant   quality assurance, speaks English, Spanish, some Japanese, studied one year of Cantonese, married, 28

Peter Becker   quality assurance, speaks English, single, 24

Mark Schultz   personnel, speaks English, studied Mandarin, 30

Work in two groups: a Luna group and a Pacific Precision group.

Part One—*Luna*

You and your group members work for Luna. You have decided that Jack Rivard should be chosen as the trainee. You must:

1. make a list of reasons why Mr. Rivard should be chosen as the trainee.

2. agree on a second choice.

Part One—*Pacific Precision*

You and your group members work for Pacific Precision. You have decided that Peter Becker should be chosen as the trainee. You must:

1. make a list of reasons why Mr. Becker should be chosen as the trainee.

2. agree on second choice.

Part Two

Now both groups should meet together. Discuss the people recommended as trainees, and choose one.

During your meetings use the correct language to show understanding, agreement and disagreement. Be aware of body language.

6 Coming to a Conclusion

UNIT FOCUS
- **Summarizing a Meeting**
- **Stating Future Tasks**
- **Ending a Meeting**

What makes someone a good meeting chairperson? Have you ever chaired a formal meeting? Was it difficult or easy?

Davis, Incorporated, an American printer manufacturer, recently selected Marin Technics to supply circuit boards for a new Davis computer. Davis and Marin Technics staff are concluding a series of meetings about the quality and design of the circuit board.

Match the words from the dialogue with the phrases on the right.

1. __ to summarize   a. a group of items

2. __ lot   b. to review the main points of a discussion

3. __ stable   c. to end a meeting or talk

4. __ to adjourn   d. not changing, constant

Compare answers with your classmates and practice using the words in sentences.

Activity 1

Jack Vargas of Marin Technics is concluding a meeting about work done to improve the Marin Technics circuit board. Joining him in the meeting are Bob Fisher and Beth Ellis of Davis.

Listen to the following dialogue and complete the missing passages.

MR. VARGAS: Before we move on, I'd like to take a moment to summarize what we've discussed so far.

MS. ELLIS: Please do.

MR. VARGAS: Mr. Cavioni and Mr. Fisher have worked together to improve our circuit board quality. [1]_____ their work, and [2]_____ they've made a very complete study of the problem.

MS. ELLIS: That's right.

MR. VARGAS: So, [3]_____ to accept their recommended changes to the basic design. [4]_____ _____ with these changes the circuit board is just about ready for production.

MR. FISHER: Yes, now there are only one or two things left to do before we can begin production.

MR. VARGAS: That's right. You at Davis [5]_____ _____ and Beth and I [6]_____ _____ to discuss the production schedule. Once we begin production [7]_____ _____ upon arrival, just until the quality becomes stable.

MS. ELLIS: [8]_____ to Marin to check on the first lot, if you like.

MR. VARGAS: That's not a bad idea. All right then, are there questions before we adjourn? Mr. Fisher, you. . . .

Summarizing a Meeting

When you come to the end of a meeting, it is good to summarize what you have said and decided.

We have decided . . .	We have decided to accept their recommended changes.
We have agreed that . . .	We have agreed that the circuit board is ready.
We've discussed . . .	We've discussed their work.

Activity 2

Review the dialogue in Activity 1 of Unit 3. Work with a partner to summarize what was said and decided in the dialogue. When you are finished, compare your summary with other people in the class.

Activity 3

Meet with a group to discuss the following problem. When you have finished, prepare a summary of the items you discussed and the decisions you made and report back to the class.

Your department at work has been assigned a special, one-year project. To complete this project on time you are going to need to hire more staff.

You would like to hire full-time employees who will become permanent members of your staff, because you expect to receive more special projects in the future. Hiring part-time employees would save you money, however.

Should you hire full-time or part-time employees? Why?

Stating Future Tasks

After you have summarized decisions and what has been said, you need to state future tasks. The language you use to introduce each task will depend upon how urgent or important it is.

> Tasks which are very important or urgent use **have to**, **need to**, **must** and **will**.
>
> *You must pass your safety testing and Beth and I need to meet again.*
>
> Tasks which are less important or urgent use **should**.
>
> *You should have all the units inspected upon arrival*
>
> Tasks which are optional use **can**.
>
> *We can send an engineer to Marin to check on the first lot, if you like.*

Activity 4

Mr Johnson is meeting with his sales staff. Listen to him describe the remaining work for the year. Fill in the tasks missing from his calendar.

October	November	December
15th: convention preparation must be completed 20th: _____ _____ _____ _____ Convention until mid-November, need to collect orders	15th: should meet to review sales progress _____ _____ _____ _____ _____	10th: _____ _____

Which tasks are the most important or urgent? Which are the least important or urgent?

Activity 5 | Meet with your group from Activity 3. Consider the solution you chose in Activity 3 and what must be done to make it successful.

1. Make a list of the tasks that must be done, and rank them from most to least important.
2. Assign the tasks to group members.

Ending a Meeting

After you summarize what has been done and what needs to be done you are ready to end your meeting. The language you use to end a meeting will depend on whether the meeting is **formal**, **informal** or **neutral**.

Activity 6 | Below is a list of expressions used to end a meeting. Mark them **F** for formal, **I** for informal or **N** for neutral.

1. ____ Well, I guess that wraps things up.

2. ____ As all items have been discussed, I suggest we adjourn.

3. ____ I believe we've covered everything.

4. ____ Let's stop here.

5. ____ I would like to suggest that we stop here.

6. ____ OK, well, that seems to be about everything.

Activity 7 | Read the following dialogues and decide whether they are formal, informal or neutral. Then fill the blanks with an appropriate expression from Activity 6 and compare your answers with those on the tape.

Dialogue A | Jack Vargas and Bob Fisher are concluding a meeting.

MR. VARGAS: Well, I'll have to check one or two points on this production schedule and then we should be ready.

MR. FISHER: Do you see any problems?

MR. VARGAS: Oh, no, don't worry about it. I'll have an answer for you very soon.

MR. FISHER: Good. Well, [1]_____.

MR. VARGAS: Thanks for coming by. I'll give you a call early next week.

MR. FISHER: Thanks, Jack. Goodbye.

MR. VARGAS: Goodbye.

Dialogue B

Mr. Webster, Jack Vargas' boss, is concluding a meeting with his staff.

MR. VARGAS: . . . and we expect to begin production for Davis in two weeks.

MR. WEBSTER: Thank you, Jack. Now, are there any last questions? Well, as all items seem to have been discussed,

2 _____. Thank you for your time, Jack, you've done an excellent job.

MR. VARGAS: Thank you, Mr. Webster.

Dialogue C

Ms. Ellis is concluding a meeting with Mr. Fisher.

MS. ELLIS: So you're happy with the way things turned out?

MR. FISHER: Yeah. Vargas is a nice guy, real easy to work with. He's going to check his schedule again and then we should be ready to start.

MS. ELLIS: That's good news. Well, 3 _____

_____. Let me know how things go.

MR. FISHER: OK. Bye-bye.

Your Turn

Your company has recently decided to hold a series of training seminars for its junior management. You and your group members have been asked to select the best seminars.

Your group has met once a week for the past month and has interviewed employees in other work sections. You now have a list of five possible seminars: 1) accounting 2) international law 3) cross-cultural training 4) finance 5) international business practice

Part One	**Part Two**
Meeting	*Summary Presentation*
Meet with your group members to select the best training seminars for Davis managers. You must:	Present the results of your first meeting to another group. Summarize what you did as a group, the decisions you made and what remains to be done. Conclude the meeting after answering any questions.
1. choose three seminars from the list of five.	
2. write a list of the tasks that must be done before the seminars can start.	
3. assign the tasks to your group members.	

Review Expressions

Asking for Opinions	How do you feel about . . . What do you think about . . . How do you feel? What do you think?
Restatement	So, what you mean is . . . In other words . . .
Entering a Conversation	Excuse me, but . . . Sorry to interrupt, but . . . Pardon me . . . Sorry for interrupting . . .
Introducing And Supporting Ideas	I think (that) . . . because . . . It seems to me (that) . . . because
Recommendations	I think we should . . . because . . .
Giving Opinions	I really think/feel that . . . I definitely think/feel . . . I think/feel . . . I tend to think/feel . . .
Explaining a Process	First . . . Second . . . Third . . . Next . . . After that . . . Finally . . .
Making Requests	We need you to . . . Could you . . . I would like you to . . . Please . . . Can you . . .
Accepting And Refusing Requests	All right. I'm sorry, I can't. I'm afraid I can't.

Agreement and Disagreement	That's what I think. Exactly. Generally I agree, but . . . I tend to agree, but . . . I don't know . . . I'm not so sure . . . I tend to disagree . . . I'm sorry, I have to disagree. I'm sorry, I can't agree with that. I'm afraid I disagree.
Showing Understanding	I see. I see your point. I understand. I see what you mean.
Summarizing a Meeting	We have decided . . . We have agreed that . . . We've discussed . . .
Ending A Meeting	I suggest we adjourn. I believe we've covered everything. I would like to suggest that we stop here. That seems to be everything. Let's stop here. I guess that wraps things up.

Answer Key and Transcripts

Unit 1

Answer Key

1. d 2. a 3. c 4. b

Activity 1

Transcript and Answer Key

MR. ITO: ... So we are planning to release this new computer series in mid-spring, around April 15. Well, ¹*what do you think* of the series? Mr. Moran?

MR. MORAN: ²*I'm quite pleased.* I especially like the portable model. You know, such a product is very important in our market and should do quite well.

MR. ITO: Mr. Garcia, ³*does this fit* well with your marketing plans?

MR. GARCIA: Yes, it does.

MR. ITO: ⁴*Which* of the models ⁵*will sell best* in Mexico?

MR. GARCIA: The first one you showed us will do well. Our customers will like the high quality.

MR. ITO: Ms. Cole, ⁶*how do you feel* about the new series?

MS. COLE: Well, frankly, I'm disappointed. We don't have anything new here. We need new technology in the US market.

MR. GARCIA: Mr. Ito, ⁷*didn't you tell us* at the last meeting that the design department was working on some new technology?

MR. ITO: Yes, they are, but development is taking more time than they expected.

MR. MORAN: Can they prepare something by spring?

MR. ITO: ⁸*No, I don't think it's possible.* Maybe if we delayed releasing the series until June ...

MS. COLE: But we can't wait. We have to introduce this new series at the trade show in March. It's the most important show of the year.

MR. ITO: I see. I'll ask design to start making changes immediately.

MR. MORAN: ⁹*How soon can they complete the changes?*

MR. ITO: I'll ask them to be finished by January. ¹⁰*What do you think,* Ms. Cole, will January be all right?

MS. COLE: That should be fine, if there aren't any delays.

Activity 2

Answer Key

Answers will vary.

1. Which languages have you studied?
2. Where are you from?
3. How often do you travel overseas?
4. How big is the company you work for?
5. What do you know about computers?

Activity 4 | *Answer Key*

Answers will vary.

1. What do you think about the new computer series?
2. How do you feel about the conference?
3. How do you feel about the new phone system?
4. What do you think about his idea?

Activity 6 | *Transcript and Answer Key*

MR. ITO: Well, Ms. Cole, the last time we met you told me about your plans for the trade show. How are your preparations going?

MS. COLE: Well, we're having a little trouble.

MR. ITO: [1]*So, what you mean is,* you're falling behind schedule?

MS. COLE: No, not yet. But we can't complete our preparations until this new series is completed. We need sample computers from this series to finish training our staff.

MR. ITO: In other words, [2]*you want those computers as soon as possible.*

MS. COLE: That's right. We'd like to receive them by January.

MR. ITO: Well, design needs time to complete their work, so I think January is too early. How do you feel about a later date?

MS. COLE: [3]*You mean* in February? The first or second week of February would be OK.

MR. ITO: All right, I'll do what I can.

MS. COLE: Thank you, I really appreciate your help.

Activity 7 | *Answer Key*

Answers will vary.

1. In other words, you've fallen behind schedule.
2. So, what you mean is, safety is important for people.
3. In other words, we should order more right away.
4. So, what you mean is, Mr. Carlson wants to see this report.
5. In other words, you want those computers as soon as possible.
6. What you mean is, she was looking for a safe car.

Unit 2

Pre-listening | *Answer Key*

1. c 2. d 3. a 4. b

Activity 1 | *Transcript and Answer Key*

MR. BOGART: I know it's difficult, but at the end of seven weeks we are going to be short 49,000 units unless you speed up your production.

MR. CHANG: [1]*How can we do this?* I don't think it's possible.

MR. BOGART: Well, you can add another work shift. By adding a shift you would . . .

MR. LEE:	[2]I'm sorry to interrupt, Mr. Bogart, but we have already done that. We've changed from a twelve-hour shift to a sixteen-hour shift. Almost all of our factory employees are working overtime.
MR. SEGAL:	[3]Excuse me, but I think I have an idea.
MR. CHANG:	[4]What do you have in mind?
MR. SEGAL:	Well, if you hire more workers you can run the plant for twenty-four hours, using three shifts.
MR. CHANG:	I'm sorry, I can't agree with that.
MR. BOGART:	[5]What's wrong with the idea? It sounds good to me.
MR. CHANG:	The problem is a matter of time. We would need time to train new workers on the machines.
MR. SEGAL:	What kind of training program do you have now?
MR. LEE:	After two days of training, each new employee works with a supervisor for two more days, before working alone.
MR. BOGART:	It might be possible to reduce training time.
MR. CHANG:	[6]How would you do that?
MR. BOGART:	We could skip the two days of supervision.
MR. CHANG:	No, I'm sorry, the supervision is too important.
MR. SEGAL:	[7]Excuse me, but [8]why can't you cut that stage?
MR. LEE:	We've found that most mistakes happen during the first week of work. Two days of supervision greatly reduces the number of mistakes.
MR. SEGAL:	But that also increases the production time.
MR. CHANG:	Yes, in the short term, but in the long term it saves time because quality is higher.

Activity 2

Answer Key

Answers will vary.

1. How can I do that?
2. What do you have in mind?
3. Why can't you agree with it?
4. How would you do that?

Activity 3

Answer Key

Answers will vary.

2. Why don't you like your job?
4. Where did you work before?
6. Who do you meet with?
8. Where have you been?
10. Where would you like to travel?

Activity 4

Answer Key

Answers will vary.

1. I'm very sorry for interrupting.
2. Forgive me for interrupting.
3. Pardon me.
4. Excuse me.

| **Activity 5** | *Answer Key* |
| | Answers will vary. |

MR. SATO:	Well, everyone in Tokyo agrees that the annual sales meeting should be in Singapore next year.
MS. BROWN:	Should we have it in November again?
MR. SATO:	If that's all right with everyone. It's a good time for us.
MR. CHEN:	[1]*Sorry to interrupt,* but why do you want the meeting in Singapore?
MS. BROWN:	Well, we had it there this year and it went very well.
MR. NAKAMURA:	Yes, the facilities were very good.
MR. LIEST:	[2]*Excuse me for interrupting,* but we were hoping that the meeting would be in Europe next year. We think that the meeting should be at a different sales office every year.
MR. SATO:	Yes, but we did have the meeting in Bonn two years ago. And Singapore is very convenient.
MR. CHEN:	[3]*Excuse me,* but what about Hong Kong? We had the meeting there four years ago and it went very well.

Activity 7

Answer Key

1. (W) 2. (I) 3. (N) 4. (A) 5. (H)

Activity 8

Transcript and Answer Key

MR. SEGAL:	I still don't understand why we can't cut the supervision stage . . .
MR. LEE:	We can't cut the two days of supervision.[1] (A)
MR. SEGAL:	But we have to cut something.[2] (W) Can we cut the training by a day and still get quality work?
MR. LEE:	Hmmm . . . . that's an option,[3] (I) but I'm afraid that cutting the training time will leave us with product defects and more delays!
MR. SEGAL:	No, I mean that instead of cutting the overall training time, we increase the supervision time to three days.
MR. LEE:	I'm sorry, I don't see your point.[4] (N)
MR. SEGAL:	I mean, we should have one day of machine training and three days of supervision. That way the workers can start production twenty-four hours earlier.
MR. LEE:	Hmmm. But I'm still worried about the quality. [5](W) If we do this, we should increase the inspection ratio.
MR. SEGAL:	Yes, that's not a bad idea.
MR. LEE:	OK. I think we have a deal.[6] (N) One day of machine training and three days of supervision.
MR. SEGAL:	Great![7] (H)

Unit 3

Pre-Listening

Answer Key

1. a 2. d 3. b 4. c

Activity 1

Transcript and Answer Key

MS. ELLIS: The DV6700 is our most important printer this year, with our newest technology. Because of this, [1]*I think that* we should make quality the most important factor in choosing a circuit board for this printer.

MR. FISHER: We've tested samples from Olsen Electronics and Marin Technics. Both samples are good, but Olsen's quality is slightly better.

MR. GREEN: [2]*It seems to me* that we also need to consider cost. How do the two companies compare?

MS. ELLIS: Both companies are offering the same price, but there is one difference. Because we are a regular customer, Olsen will be very flexible with their production schedule. [3]*I think* we should choose Olsen, [4]*because* their price is OK and we need the flexibility they offer.

MR. FISHER: Olsen? But we always have problems with Olsen when we use them. There are production delays . . .

MR. GREEN: Yes, but according to your test data, Olsen's quality is better than Marin Technics'.

MR. FISHER: I said that the Olsen circuit board is slightly better. Frankly, [5]*I think* that Marin Technics is the best choice, [6]*because* our engineers can always give them some instructions for improvements.

MR. GREEN: Well, [7]*it seems to me* that it would be a lot easier to use Olsen, like we did before.

MR. FISHER: No, [8]*I think we should* use Marin Technics, [9]*because* their quality can be improved, their price is good and they won't give us any holdups like Olsen always does.

MS. ELLIS: Hmmm, [10]*I think you're right.* Also, if we do decide to use the DV6700 circuit board in our other models, Marin should be able to . . .

Activity 3

Answer Key

1. A: I think <u>we should buy this computer</u> because the price is just right.
   B: But prices might drop again soon, so I think <u>we should wait</u>.
2. A: Because Mr. Burne is leaving tomorrow, <u>we should talk with him today</u>.
   B: OK, <u>but we shouldn't take a lot of his time</u> because he's very busy.

Activity 5

Answer Key

_3_ I feel that you haven't studied this enough.
_1_ I definitely think they will agree.
_5_ I tend to feel that it's a good idea.
_2_ I really feel that she will like this.
_4_ I think this is a good report.

Transcript and Answer Key

MR. VARGAS: Jack Vargas speaking.

MS. ELLIS: Jack, this is Beth Ellis from Davis. I have some good news for you. We've finished our evaluation and have decided to use your circuit board.

MR. VARGAS: Great! How large an order will you need?

MS. ELLIS: Before we do that, there are a few conditions we need to discuss.

MR. VARGAS: OK.

MS. ELLIS: The first condition concerns production. How do you feel about giving us a more flexible production schedule?

MR. VARGAS: Well, [1]*I think that would be all right.* We've done that sort of thing before.

MS. ELLIS: Good. Our other concern is the quality. We'd like you to accept some technical instructions from our engineers. What do you think?

MR. VARGAS: Hmmm. [2]*I tend to feel* there'll be some problems. Can we set up a meeting between your engineering staff and mine? [3]*I really think* we should discuss this.

MS. ELLIS: [4]*I think that's a good idea.* And listen, Jack, don't worry too much about this. [5]*I definitely feel* we've made the right choice by selecting Marin Technics. [6]*I think that* after a few minor changes we'll have a fine product.

MR. VARGAS: I'm happy to hear you say that. Let's look at our calendars and set up that meeting . . . .

Unit 4

Answer Key

1. d 2. a 3. b 4. c

Transcript and Answer Key

MR. ITO: . . . Those are the new products and their features. Now I'd like us to discuss our preparation for the upcoming trade show. Ms. Baker?

MS. BAKER: Thank you, Mr. Ito. We have four steps to complete today. [1]*First,* we need to assign tasks; who will be responsible for which activities. [2]*Then* we need to discuss how much room each product will have. [3]*For our third step,* I'd like us to break up and work in groups for a few hours. [4]*Finally,* I'd like to meet again this afternoon to discuss our progress. Any questions? All right, let's start with the assignments. Ms. Cole, we'd like you to take care of the personal computer display.

MS. COLE: [5]*I'm sorry, but I can't.* I have to be in New York at that time. I'd like to have Mr. Ford take my place.

MS. BAKER: Mr. Ford, is that all right with you?

MR. FORD: [6]*Yes, that's fine.*

MS. BAKER: Mr. Ito, *⁷could you work with him?*
MR. ITO: Sure.
MS. BAKER: OK, Ms. Meyer, *⁸we need you to organize* the printer team.
MS. MEYER: *⁹Yes, of course.* My staff has already started preparations.
MS. BAKER: Good. All right, last on the list is systems products. Mr. Miller, I'd like you to take care of that.
MR. MILLER: *¹⁰All right.* Can Mr. Phillips work with me?
MS. BAKER: Oh, yes, that's a good idea.

Activity 2

Answer Key

A. 3 B. 2 C. 5 D. 1 E. 4

Transcript

First someone has to set up the display area shelves and tables. Then we move our products to the display area and set them up. The third step is the most important. We have to make sure that everything works properly. We don't want anything to break down while the customer is watching! Next we have to set up an information table of pamphlets and catalogs. The final step is very difficult for me. We have to arrange food for the customers!

Activity 5

Answer Key

Answers will vary.

1. Excuse me, could I borrow a pen?
2. I need you to finish this report for me.
3. I would like you to teach me some Spanish.
4. Can you lend me some money for lunch?
5. Can you explain this software to me?

Activity 6

Transcript and Answer Key

MR. ITO: Ms. Baker, can you help me?
MS. BAKER: *¹Yes, of course.* What can I do for you?
MR. ITO: I have to buy some souvenirs to take back to Japan, and I don't know what to buy. I need you to give me some advice.
MS. BAKER: Sure. *²Who are they for?*
MR. ITO: My co-workers.
MS. BAKER: OK. Well, California wine is one idea.
MR. ITO: That sounds nice. Can you recommend a special brand?
MS. BAKER: *³I'm afraid I can't.* I don't know much about wine. You should ask Ms. Cole.
MR. ITO: OK, I'll do that. There is one more thing. I'd like you to get everyone together for a short meeting this afternoon.
MS. BAKER: *⁴I'm sorry but I can't.* Both Mr. Ford and Ms. Cole are out this afternoon. Could you make it tomorrow morning?
MR. ITO: *⁵All right.* That'll be fine.

Unit 5

Answer Key

1. c 2. d 3. b 4. a

Activity 1

Transcript and Answer Key

MR. BOGART: This watch has been very popular, so we'd like you to supply an additional 100,000 units this month.

MR. CHANG: [1]*I see.* That's good news for us, but there is one problem.

MR. BOGART: What's that?

MR. CHANG: This increased schedule we're running has caused production costs to increase. At our last inspection we found that defects have doubled.

MR. BOGART: Well, [2]*I understand* your situation but your new workers should know their jobs by now. You shouldn't have any more problems.

MR. CHANG: [3]*I'm afraid I can't agree.* Even if the workers improve, we can only hope to break even on this new order.

MR. BOGART: But if you increase your price we'll have to increase ours and we'll both lose business.

MR. CHANG: [4]*We understand,* but we can't continue with the current situation.

MR. BOGART: There has to be something we can do to solve this problem.

MR. CHANG: Well, if you can give us a larger order, about 200,000 units, then we can keep our price low for you.

MR. BOGART: An extra 100,000? No, I'm sorry. I mean, [5]*I see your point,* but [6]*I'm afraid I can't agree with that right now.*

MR. CHANG: How about air freight? If you pay for air freight, we can return to our normal production schedule and still deliver the order on time.

MR. BOGART: No, I'm sorry, [7]*I have to disagree with that.* The cost is too high.

Activity 2

Answer Key

1. __D__ I tend to disagree . . .
2. __B__ Generally I agree, but . . .
3. __E__ I'm sorry, I have to disagree.
4. __A__ Exactly.
5. __C__ I'm not so sure . . .
6. __C__ I don't know . . .
7. __E__ I'm afraid I disagree . . .
8. __A__ That's what I think.
9. __B__ I tend to agree, but . . .
10. __E__ I'm sorry, I can't agree with that.

Activity 5

Answer Key (US and Britain)

1. The speaker is relaxed and wants others to be relaxed.
2. The speaker is angry or intent.
3. The listener is pleased.
4. The listener is interested.
5. The listener is bored.

Activity 6

Answer Key

1. B   2. E   3. A   4. C   5. D

Unit 6

Pre-Listening

Answer Key

1. b   2. a   3. d   4. c

Activity 1

🔲

Transcript and Answer Key

MR. VARGAS: Before we move on, I'd like to take a moment to summarize what we've discussed so far.

MS. ELLIS: Please do.

MR. VARGAS: Mr. Cavioni and Mr. Fisher have worked together to improve our circuit board quality. [1]*We've discussed* their work, and [2]*we have agreed that* they've made a very complete study of the problem.

MS. ELLIS: That's right.

MR. VARGAS: So, [3]*we have decided* to accept their recommended changes to the basic design. [4]*We've all agreed that* with these changes the circuit board is just about ready for production.

MR. FISHER: Yes, now there are only one or two things left to do before we can begin production.

MR. VARGAS: That's right. You at Davis [5]*must pass your safety tests* and Beth and I [6]*need to meet again* to discuss the production schedule. Once we begin production [7]*you should have all the units inspected* upon arrival, just until the quality becomes stable.

MS. ELLIS: [8]*We can also send an engineer* to Marin to check on the first lot, if you like.

MR. VARGAS: That's not a bad idea. All right then, are there questions before we adjourn? Mr. Fisher, you . . . .

Activity 4

🔲

Transcript

Looking at the next three months, I see a very busy schedule. All preparations for the October sales convention must be completed by the fifteenth of that month. At the convention on the twentieth *you should begin to collect sales orders,* and from the convention until mid-November we all need to work very hard to collect orders. On the fifteenth of November, we should meet to review our sales progress. *We can change our sales plans at that time* if necessary. Mr. Beckwith from the head office is visiting in the beginning of December. *We have to present our sales report to him* on the tenth, *so you should all begin writing your reports* in November.

Answer Key

October	November	December
15th: convention preparation must be completed 20th: *should begin to collect sales orders* convention until mid-November, need to collect orders	15th: should meet to review sales progress *can change sales plans* *begin writing reports*	10th: *present sales reports to Mr. Beckwith*

Activity 6

Answer Key

1. I   2. F   3. N   4. N-I   5. F   6. N-I

Activity 7

Transcript and Answer Key

Answers will vary.

A: Neutral

MR. VARGAS:	Well, I'll have to check one or two points on this production schedule and then we should be ready.
MR. FISHER:	Do you see any problems?
MR. VARGAS:	Oh, no, don't worry about it. I'll have an answer for you very soon.
MR. FISHER:	Good. Well, ¹*that seems to be everything.*
MR. VARGAS:	Thanks for coming by. I'll give you a call early next week.
MR. FISHER:	Thanks, Jack. Goodbye.
MR. VARGAS:	Goodbye.

B: Formal

MR. VARGAS:	. . . and we expect to begin production for Davis in two weeks.
MR. WEBSTER:	Thank you, Jack. Now, are there any last questions? Well, as all items seem to have been discussed, ²*I suggest we adjourn.* Thank you for your time, Jack, you've done an excellent job.
MR. VARGAS:	Thank you, Mr. Webster.

C: Informal

MS. ELLIS:	So you're happy with the way things turned out?
MR. FISHER:	Yeah. Vargas is a nice guy, real easy to work with. He's going to check his schedule again and then we should be ready to start.
MS. ELLIS:	That's good news. Well, ³*I guess that wraps things up.* Let me know how things go.
MR. FISHER:	OK, Bye-bye.